Rain[illegible]ows
&
Sunsets

Poems by

Karon Adela Galloway

First published in paperback by
Michael Terence Publishing in 2023
www.mtp.agency

ISBN 9781800946217

Love has no colour or gender, it's just a feeling…

Contents

The Wishing Stone 1
At The Bottom of The Garden 2
Children 3
Dancing with Pixies 4
Who Are We Supposed To Be? 5
Hardened Hands to Soften 7
Buttercups And Dandelions 8
Sharing a Moment 9
Laundry Dollies 10
Beautific 12
Raindrops 13
A Sweet Memory 14
Red Eye 15
Pebbles 16
Rainbows & Sunsets 17
Ugly stockings 18
My Weakening Xiphoid 19
Mother 20
13 Rooms 21
Comfort Loan Zone 23

Soul Ties 24
Lost in Transit 25
Coffee and Nicotine 26
Hearts Felt Passing 27
Lady Birds 28
When Nature Cries She Roars 29
No Trousseau 30
Mermaids 31
Awake 32
Checking In 33
The Bitch 34
Halloween 35
Midnight 36
The Dolphin Call 37
In My Prowess 38
What Filch! 39
Unicorns and Butterflies 40
The Beach 41
Love 42
Plug Me In! 43
You Square 44
Common Place 45

Little Black Dress 46
Melodic People 47
Hearts Felt Passing 48
Impartial Forgiveness 49
My Blank Wall Day 50
Maturity 52
Egress 54
As He Rests 55
One 56
The Struggle 58
The Anorak Man 60
The Lion the Witch and The Wardrobe 62
Women 63
Forget You Not 65
Key-Mo-Xy 66
Dancer 67
Daddy Archer 68
Men 69
Labels 70
A Million Dollars 71
The Launderette 72
Feeling Fed up Again! 73

When The Wind Blows ... 75
Amsterdam Oak & Fan ... 76
A Good Day ... 77
Angels ... 78
Drum & Bass ... 79
Who Are You? ... 80
The Witnesses ... 81
The Boy from Marz ... 82
SEX ... 83
When The Night Calls ... 84
Dreams ... 85
Warriors ... 87
Lacuna ... 89
Grounded Stars ... 90
Changing Face ... 92
The Tree ... 94
Yesteryears ... 95
Lachrymose ... 96
Honey Bees ... 97
When He Comes ... 98
Distant Dreaming ... 100
Rainbows & Sunsets ... 102

The Wishing Stone

I was about aged five
And I went to a huge forest
With the Sunday school from church
Some elderly people and florists

At the top of the Wrekin
Was a wishing stone
And I may have just told
Someone at home

That a dancing ballerina jewellery box
Was what I would wish for
So I closed my eyes
and wished for even more

A few weeks later
There was a knock on the door
At home
I felt dizzy inside
Because I was all alone

Then upstairs in my bedroom
There was this jewellery box
With a beautiful dancer
Wearing a pretty blue frock.

At The Bottom of The Garden

At the bottom of the garden
Under a forest of trees
Is a whole different world
That only fairy people see

It's an underground haven
Full of sparkles and pretty things
With hand woven blankets
There are no such thing as machines

Where only fairy people
Can venture in
Or those who are not judgemental
And full of sin

Where only fairy people
Who care for the land and tree's
And protect the woodland forest
And keep away from dead flees.

Children

Some short
Some tall
Some children
Never make it
Over the wall

Some fight
Some win
Some sheltered
From adult sin

Some outspoken
Some shy
Some bully
Some cry

All different shades of skin
From light to dark
Every child born has the right to live
Every adult living has the right to give

Time and understanding
And a listening ear
Every child in our universe
Has no right to fear.

Dancing with Pixies

Entering a twilight zone
Bodies pulsating
To the heavy base box
Bodies exaggerating
Gyrating to solid sounds
From the overground
And underground

Lights flashing
Teeth chattering
Speed, weed, dope, cocaine
Ecstasy, ketamine
Can't be good for the brain
Takes the pain away
For several hours
Hands swaying above heads
Imitating mystical powers

Kissing your mate in sensual drive
Pressing bodies touching hot,
Pouting behinds
Sweat, adrenalin, racing hearts
Looking forward to the next rave
fast sex and fast cars.

Who Are We Supposed To Be?

What's going on in the world?
Who are we supposed to be!
Technology, evolution, the net
And what about the sea?

Plastic pollution, wars, floods,
Guns, knives
Youths in hoodies
Even mine

Crime at it's peak
Homelessness in the streets
Plastic celebrities
Some they are kind
Saving bees

And what about the trees
Chop, chop, chop them down
Then plant some more
Refugees sleeping
On cold floors

Mental health at the forefront
I guess it's about time
The rich getting richer
Drinking the Devil's wine

Who are we supposed to be
Where does this all lead?
We are under so much pressure
To succeed

I got a pound in my pocket
And a hole in my shoe
A bit of money in the bank
They say that money rules

My Bible all dusty
As I say it's difficult to read it
Some people are really fanatic
And only breathe it

Who are we supposed to be
Where are we supposed to go?
What are we supposed to do?
Does the government really know?

Some people have it easy
Some have it hard
You know it's like a jungle
In my back yard!

Hardened Hands to Soften

Holding, touching, feeling
A warm hot squeeze
Caressing, clench, knead, stroke
Pull, lead, gently
Protect, seal, you…

Buttercups And Dandelions

Flowers are everywhere
In every season
All colours of the rainbow
And even when the land
Is full of snow
I bet you can find a flower
Shining or withering away
Flowers always grow
And in the spring time
When my garden is full of buttercups
I wish they would always stay
Simple flowers of yellow
That shine throughout the day
I dare not crush them
With my clumsy feet
Especially when I dance at night
I can imagine a spread of buttercups
All happy and fine
Then springs up dandelions
And a duel begins at nine
Buttercups and dandelions
Swinging and swaying under the moon
Or in the morning dew
When other flowers bloom.

Sharing a Moment

Sharing a moment
Is a moment shared
Even when your alone
And feeling scared

Sharing a moment
Is a sacred moment in time
Whether you are yours
Or you are mine

Sharing a moment
Is a moment found
Whether in darkness
Or light
Or silent sound

Sharing a moment
Is a moment free
And that's how moments
Are supposed to be.

Laundry Dollies

Rise and shine
We awake
To wash your clothes
Doesn't matter
Who you are
Or what lies
Between your toes

Washing your
Clothes clean
And your dirty underwear
Because we are not stuck up
No we don't care
Rather therapeutic
Folding hundreds
Of pairs of socks
And we find it quite funny
When other women
Don't' wash their own
Fancy frocks!

And mothering others
Is what we do best
But don't ever try to
Underestimate us

Then after our work is done
For a little pocket money
Some of us return home
To play wonder super mummy

So the next time you see a Dolly
You better shake her hand
Because every laundry Dolly
Is in very much demand!

Beautific

To hold you gently against my flesh
Innocent, tiny and wise
The sound of your first cries
Did not bother me at all
And when you slept quietly
I wondered how you came to be from me.

Raindrops

Raindrops on my weary face
Sun shines when I'm feeling out of place

Snow falls and I feel like ice
The wind blows and I might take a slice

Of him, to taste on my lips
His fine soft skin against my hips

Rain drops on my fuzzy head
My love roars when he is feeling dread

The sun shines when we are two
I can only say this for a few

Wind blows when we walk
And the stars shine when we talk

Rain drops on my toes
Snow falls and the wind blows

Sun shines and he is mine
Rain pours and we feel fine.

A Sweet Memory

Your mahogany skin to touch
Is like soft leather
And as you embraced me
I took you in to the beat of a drum
Hearts pounding
Pouring sweat on my brow
I did taste you
Like hot chocolate
Silky, smooth
And ever so sweet.

Red Eye

Your red eye
Only see's one part of me
A part that only
You can see

Torn, tattered and bleeding
From my heart
I pour out patterns
Only you can see.

Pebbles

My scars are just a reminder
That even in the darkness
I am whole
And when the light shined
Once again
I did dance under the moon
Yesterday I remembered the thunder
As it roared and I soared
To greater heights
And the pebbles they just balanced
As I settled for more
Than less of you.

Rainbows & Sunsets

Raindrops fall
Like a cascade of candy
On green grass
Wet beneath my feet
Soft to the touch
Blades of grass
Get stuck between my toes
The cotton ball clouds
Shift above the blue skies
And the sun takes a peak
A rainbow forms
And the distance is too long
To collect my pot of gold
The rain stops and I wait silently
Dreaming of the moon
But never forgetting
The sun which set down after raindrops
Which washed away my fears.

Ugly stockings

Fish net
Fishing
Covered
Over
Fleshy bones
Fixed together
Covering joints
Thick and torn
Like joints of meat
Feet
Covered by
Fishnet stockings
Worn and torn
Covering scars
Torn and hard
Worn
Flunky
Phished net
Feat!

My Weakening Xiphoid

Like a rod
With pointed tip
Fishing fish
With hands clasped
Ready for action
At random
Being revived
To stand tall
Wistful wounded
My blood drops droplets
From an adaptation
Of what I still don't understand,
Me.

Mother

Mother I remembered our long walks
The sun shining on our face
I took notice of our long talks
To me you were fallen from grace

You growing older and weary you had become bitter
I wanted only good things for you
I wondered if it helped if I were your sitter
To you I always wanted to stay true

You set me free and we fell separate
I know you loved me in your own special way
I wanted to help you I was desperate
I was always hoping for better days

So now I look to the sky and hope
You are at rest
I know you loved me in your darkest hours
Still you did nothing but your best.

13 Rooms

Take a list
Look through it
Take the lift
Do my shift
Run around
Make the beds
Absent rooms
Absent beds

Check the list
Count the heads
Stand in line
Take my meds
Look at me
I can dance
Got a figure
Change it's stance

Keep your list
Hold your tongue
Stick it out
When I've done wrong

Take my meds
Hold my thoughts
Keep your patience
From getting worse

Forcing out
A temper chant
Watch me giggle
Watch me skank

I can flaunt
Keep me up
Keep me in
I am tough

Hold me down
Hold my chin
Check your list
Play to win

Count your heads
While I stand in line
I take your meds
While you take my time.

Comfort Loan Zone

No thrills
Sitting slumped
Feet chilled
Cookies crunched
Snacks all day
Food of plenty
Slopped on platters
Then stomachs empty
Stay locked in all day
Smoked at break away
Pills at bed time
Then morning awake
Repeat the day
For heavens sake
A display of affection
And a listening ear
For someone to tell you
"I love you dear".

Soul Ties

My flesh profits nothing
The persistence
Of my discipline
Overcomes resistance
Lingering and wandering
About old flames
And friends
Who have never really left me

But are just on their flight
With all my might
I fight to walk
And forever breaking free
Of the ties that once
Entrapped me.

Lost in Transit

Wake up, wake up
Early to their call
A shuffling of feet
Along the corridor

Swallow, swallow
Not a bird in flight
A tantrum and a squabble
A real bitch fight

Waiting and waiting
For time to pass
All women squashed together
From all different class

Wanting and waiting
To be let out
A new beginning on the horizon
A new stance
A new pout.

Coffee and Nicotine

Early morning rise
I despise
The fluttering
In my gut
And knowing
For a period of time
I am just stuck in a rut

I head for the machine
Whilst every women in the unit
Is in deep dreams

To make my sweet coffee
To go with my nicotine
As I inhale stale tobacco
They are a combination
Of feeling unclean.

Hearts Felt Passing

Mix and matching colour
From a rainbow
Flowing and intertwining
Joining minds enveloping
Coping with life's timelines
Stuck flat on a landscape
Of wishful thinking
Thoughts of yesterdays
Hearts felt sinking
Passages of shapes and figures
Not all perfect
But worth the weight in freight
In light shades
Which shadow the passing ship
We once both occupied
With thoughts of freedom.

Lady Birds

Tall, slim, slender
Trans gender
Feminine flirty
Or shirty skirty
Long hair straight
Bent or curled
Or too short showing
A defined rigid shape
Dresses sparkles
High pitch tone voice
From hormone treatment
To street club fame
Then home alone
To family shame
Tall slim, slender
Aphrodite or plain
Transgender.

When Nature Cries She Roars

Earth quakes, disaster
Rain pours and there after
Lives taken, broken lost and confused
Amongst the poor or rich or misused

In places the sea levels are rising
Soon in years, many populations will be lost
With new island built
At a very high cost

Ice caps melting and gases rising high
Microchips put in wheely bins
To decrease the rubbish
Rotten and dry

Life is not just a token of money
To heat a cold room
Or electric to charge the light
Once a child has left it's mothers womb

When we realize the world is over populated
Where we need to come together
Without spawning more
Then perhaps God and his Angels
Can somehow create a new world without hatred and wars.

No Trousseau

No trousseau
For my kind
Only for he
That is blind
To see straight through me
If he could
And could I ever
Be understood?
No trousseau
To look back at me
To see me walk
So gallantly
No trousseau
For the disturbed or poor
And no trousseau
For the aging boar
No trousseau
For me I think
Still sailing on my ship
Which I hope don't sink
With all my jewels
And dreams and hope
I don't need a trousseau
For me to cope.

Mermaids

All eyes on you
All eyes on me
Octopuses floating
In the deep blue sea

Dolphins play
And crabs do claw
Sea horses bobbing
And mermaids ashore

Awake

I am awake again, again
Still having a paper and pen
Not the kind of paper
You write on
Rather the paper
you turn the electricity on

Not the kind of pen
You write with
But rather the kind of pen
You sit in

At present all cosy and calm
And a little bit tired
Not fucked up, depressed and wired.

Awake, awake, awake, I be
And I still can't tell you
All I've seen

I tried before but they say
I'm insane
Been luck so far
To not get a bullet to my brain

So I'll wait in silence
In stern and stealth
And focus yet again
On my mental health!

Checking In

Just checking in
And not yet out
Surely that day
Will come without
A doubt

Gotta get by
And let my demons
To rest
Before another fucker
Try and put me to a test

Gotta praise high
And not too low
And never let the sad man
Reap what he know

For all in us are good
Even though sometimes we're bad
And all of us are worthy
Even though we're all mad.

The Bitch

I love the water
But it doesn't like me much
Especially when it's cold to the touch
The sea want's to pull me in
And drag me in
Deep, deep down
Even though I can swim
With it's sharks and octopuses
So horrid and tame
Wanting me to play their game
So I say on land or sky
Is where I be
Amongst the stars or sitting under a tree
For I have a heart that beats like a drum
And when it stops beating
Only then she's won!

Halloween

Bones rattle beneath
Silken robe
Blood drops droplets
From crooked nose

Hair of wire
Tangled beneath
Tall black hat

Broomsticks and
bed knobs
and hallows
black cat.

Midnight

After midnight the cats
They roam from home to home
And the dogs rest
Their weary head
In my bed
I stir, then up to rise once more
For I got chores
And they are never ending.

The Dolphin Call

Swimming in the sea
Playing together merrily
Feeding their offspring
With plenty of fish
And never too greedy
What a tasty dish!

Always sharing
and caring with glee
You can hear their calls
echo out at sea

Beckoning to come play
And watch them dance
When you are given
Half the chance

Swimming and laughing
In the sea
The sweetest kindest dolphins
So let's go see!

In My Prowess

Take time to walk
Take time to think
Take time to remember
Take time to wink

Take time to listen
Take time to nudge
Take time to forget
Or bare a grudge

Take time to make love
Take time to please
Especially when you
Feel at ease

Take time to love
And take time to be kind
But never ever
Change your mind.

What Filch!

Don't filch my heart
Don't filch my mind
For I am not stupid
And I am not blind

Don't filch my body
Or filch my sex
Because if you do
I will be surely vexed

Don't filch my voice
Or filch my love
Because if you do
I will have to shove

And lead you
into the light
And away from the dark
So you don't have to hear
The mad dog's bark.

Unicorns and Butterflies

Galloping across the fields
With long mane swaying in the wind
Trampling on pretty daisies
As birds chirp and sing

Butterflies flapping
their multicoloured wings
in the sunlight
while unicorns try to pass them
out of sight

to shade themselves from the sun
still the butterflies dance has begun
on a hazy day in the Sunkist breeze
to make way for the unicorn
to gallop at ease.

The Beach

She left her country when she could
Away from the hustle of the fevala hood

From the beach hourly is where she saved
Man after man she was their slave

Making money through her sex
Looking back with no regrets

From the slums is where she grew
With no education, what else could she do?

And now she's older with no children in sight
She doesn't know where they are, still she fight

They're somewhere in this world, she knows still
With children of their own, and pockets to fill.

Love

Love is never easy
But it can be kind
Love can be blind
And when it comes
And when it goes
We are left bewildered
On our tippy toes!

Plug Me In!

Plug me in when you feel low
Then I will show you
What you need to know

Switch me on when you feel nice
And not feeling
as cold as ice

Plug me in
 when you want to surrender
Or when you want
To go on a bender.

You Square

Between my fingers
I knit you square
Darning a blanket
To cover him and keep him warm

He was cold, shivering
Fed up, curled up
By my window left open
For a crisp breeze

How I ached for winter to return
So we could crunch our feet
On slushy snow
To and fro beckoning
For cosy nights in
When our lights would be dim

Then we could have
Each other
And nothing could tear us
Apart.

Common Place

Whatever the colour
Whatever the race
We all survive
In common place

Whatever the shape
Whatever the size
We all shall come
To our demise

But while we love
and learn and give
our hearts beat to a rhythm
that's how we live

So keep thankful
For every breath we take
As our journey on earth
Is worth the break.

Little Black Dress

Got a little black dress
For only three pounds
Gonna wear my black dress
When no one is around

Got a little black number
To show off my legs
And my breasts and butt
Away from the dreads

Got a little black dress
For my man to see
And maybe if I'm lucky
He takes me out to tea

Got a little black dress
For when the sun does shine
Gonna wear it with my gold locket
And my beautiful chimes.

Melodic People

People passing
Swaying to and fro
People running away
From what they know

Bodies pulsating
To the rhythm of a beat
People busy hustling
In the streets

Bodies touching
And passing by
People gasping
And wondering why?

Short and tall
Fat and thin
Moving in a trance
With every limb

Walking and talking
In a melodic stance
Swinging and swaying
Just like a dance

Bodies rushing
With hearts beating in tune
To the sun rays that shine on us
Or to the silence of the moon.

Hearts Felt Passing

Mix and matching colours
From a rainbow
Flowing and intertwining
Joining minds, enveloping
And coping with life's time lines
Stuck flat on a landscape
Of wishful thinking
Thoughts of yesterdays
Hearts felt sinking
Passages of figures and shapes
All not perfect
But worth the weight and freight
In light shades
That shadow
The passing ship
That we both once occupied
With thoughts
Of freedom.

Impartial Forgiveness

In winds of uncertainty
Your forgiven without a doubt
Whilst a butterfly dances
Around twigs and branches
I watch and surmount

Only memories keep me steady
In the dominance of the night
And now I take flight putting
Wrongs to right

Never forgetting
As I don't care to forget
And turn all my negative heart felt pains
Into thoughts and feelings
Of pure love

And appreciation
That I am here now
Forever in your heart
Still free with unshakeable breath.

My Blank Wall Day

Some money gone
And a baby too
She's feeling lonely
Fed up and blue
No heating
Electricity gone
Her line is cut off
She can't call her mom
She see's the doctor
Maybe once a week
He looks her over
She still can't sleep
The medication it make her numb
Her heart is racing
It's my blank wall day
That's what she replied
With a bottle of whisky
And blood shot eyes
It's my blank wall day
And I feel alive
With a bottle of whisky
And eyes rolling
Nobody visits to comfort me

Only weeds in the garden
For my neighbours to see
I'll plant sunflowers
Before I'm dead
I need more whisky
To take me to bed
It's my blank wall day
Thar's what she replied
With a bottle of whisky
And blood shot eyes
It's my blank wall day
And I feel alive
With a bottle of whisky
And eyes rolling.

Maturity

No more screams
And shouting
I'll be patient
And more understanding

Like a ripened fruit
Ready to pick
I shall stay calm
And listen when I'm spoken to
Not answer back in alarm

It takes a mature person
For me too, to be mature
Not me treated like some
Screwed up wench or hoar
You know a pregnant teenager
Can be a child and too also mature
inside running emotionally wild

Though a woman can be
Quite a baby too
It's only adult childish men
Like them to be that way, few

Maturity is physically grown
And really being mature
Emotionally and mentally
Set by the law

Mature can also mean
A payment is due
Because if you want to
I'll charge you too!

Our elders can understand
That they can learn from us
And whatever the generation
We can find something to discuss

Maturity is emotional and mental balance
And understanding
What is right from what is wrong
Like a ripened mellow fruit
Fully developed and strong

Someone who can carry their own weight
And the weight of others too
A heavy weight on one's shoulders
A heavy weight just like me and you!

Egress

Seven meters above ground
I did not fall forward
Flat on my face
I fell backwards.
Into a pile of leaves
Cushioning me in the dark
Then I got up
And walked to a bus stop
And waited for my ride
With night demons.

As He Rests

As he rests
I'm wide awake
From him to me
My heart does ache

And when he's not Around me
I occasionally fall
And get all anxious
When he doesn't call.

One

He asked me to marry him
Of course I said yes
Maybe one day
I might just wear that white dress

We have a dog between us
Instead of a son
He confessed to me
That I am the one

Sometimes we argue
Sometimes we fight
I try to live alone
With all my might

But when I am free
To do as I please
My heart is lonely
And not at ease

He makes me mad
He twists me up
He calms me down
When I'm mistook

Maybe we met
In another life?
Makes me feel a little anxious
To think I could someday be his wife

We are quite similar
Him and me
We live in our own world with our pup
Just us three

We both have callas
We both have scars
I know he was sent to me
Straight from mars!

We both struggle sometimes
And have had an eventful life
We are just hoping for better days
Instead of all the strife

So if we ever make it
To be one and for all
I'll be right by his side to catch him
In case he does fall.

The Struggle

Some people find it hard
To make ends meet
Some people work for a little
Some people live on the streets

Drug use or depression
Or drinking to numb the pain
All easy to access
But not too good for the brain

Our children growing
At a steady rate
And parents forever worrying
If we can steer them straight

Along their path
It may be like a winding road
To who knows where
With their heavy load

On our children's shoulders
A weight just like you and me
Hoping they can handle
adult responsibilities

There is so much pressure
To make it in this life
In our ever changing world
With all it's struggle and strife

Us parents try and try
But we can not do everything right
Still the best we can do is
 encourage our children
to never give up the fight.

The Anorak Man

With his ruck sac on his back
And stripy jumper in tac
Tucked into his high waist jeans
Rather scruffy and no looking
Like a ken doll dream

His short hair all messy
And a stubble on his chin
Just a bit of baby hair
To match his cheeky grin

Just wandering the streets
On a cloudy day
With no map in his hands
To find his way

People rushing and passing him by
They don't give a shit
His feet tired from wandering the streets
It's time now for him to sit

On something soft and cosy
And warm with a meal
He's got many more tomorrows
To beg borrow and steal

With a pound in his pocket
That is all he has got
For a strong can of larger
We may have forgot

That yesterday he was someone
With a degree or maybe a phd
When time get's tough
This could happen to you or me

A breakdown in relationships
Or a loss of a job
A loss of a friend
A loss of a dog

In any kind of weather
We could lose ourselves
So be kind to a stranger
That is what the good book tells!

The Lion the Witch and The Wardrobe

At the back of the wardrobe
Is just wood
And flat at the wall
This is understood

The witch opens the wardrobe
And takes a peek in
All they are is fancy clothes
Wich look rather grimme

The lion beckons to her call
Even when she thinks she has it all
The lion roars in her ear
Even though she has no fear
Of the wood
That is flat at the back of the wall
Even when she thinks
She has it all!

Women

Some women are lovely
Some women are ace
All different figures
From all different race

Short or tall
Curvy or slim
Some with large breasts
Or perky or flat
Oval faced or double chin

Some women can look all pretty
In front of your face
Some women filled with jealousy
Some women are not ace

I came from a woman she was my mum
I knew she wished I was her son
Some women feminine and sweet
Or butch and hard
Or drugged up on streets

And hoar themselves out
To get rid of their pains
From when they were abused
Again and again

Some women live the struggle
Yet have to be strong

Some women never have children
And wished they belonged

But if you are a woman
And you give all that you can
Be proud to be a woman
Because it's hard to be a man.

Forget You Not

Your lacking in memory
You may have forgotten about me
The little girl you took in
After just the age three

Your memory may have faded
But would you remember my voice?
This dementia can hit us at anytime
As we just don't have a choice

And like my aunty Christine
Who just withered away
She too lost her memory
And couldn't find her way

With the love a family to shelter
And make their way at ease
It's the little things that help them
To remember as they please.

Key-Mo-Xy

My first came out like a lion
With a loud cry and a roar
All wise and precious
I was ever so proud and more

The second I abandoned
As she was a surprise to me
As I was young and exhausted
And under a lot of scrutiny

The third my little Angle
And now all fully grown
Those three came from me
Even now far from home

I wonder if they will ever have children
and make me a Nanna one day
So I can create beautiful memories
And watch them laugh and play.

Dancer

It all started when I was about age five
Dancing to the Top 40
With my family by my side

Then as I grew older
Dancing to disco and pop
My hair a little afro
In peddle pushers not a frock

I later went to dance school
And began tap and disco too
Then around aged twelve
I was on a big performing in front of a few

At seventeen I went to performing arts school
And did all different types of dance
Then later in clubs and on television
And on videos when given half the chance

I had my own group at one stage
And choreographed some strange moves
Then later a stripper around a pole
Dancing Infront of many men and fools

But now I just dance at parties
When I'm drunk or high on weed
Or at home when I'm all alone
To my tunes when I'm feeling free.

Daddy Archer

I know it's nearly time
And you don't have much of it left
Until you take your last and final breath

I will never ever forget you
And what you meant to me
You taught me about God
when I was younger
you showed me how to be free

You taught me the game of football
and how to be part of a team
your big garden you attended
it was just a children's dream

I felt safe around you
Because you were full of light
I know sometimes I made you angry
And often there was a fight

Because I played up towards your mrs
And made her blood boil
While she too was under much strife
But she too stayed very loyal

Before it is the end of you
I'll remember all the love you gave me
And how you showered me with your presence
And also taught me how to be free.

Men

So far I have met many
Different lovers from all corners
Of the world
Some soft and feminine
Or hard and obscured
Some that have been a gay closet
Some violent and thick
Some that have put me under a lot of pressure
Some that have made me sick
Like the one I got away from
Jumping out of his running car
It smelt of rotten flesh
And I surly did run far
Another who hated me appreciating women
Because he himself loved men
Now he's fled far, far up the country
To build another den
I know it can be difficult
When you've left your mothers womb
Your all so busy building battleships
And sending people to the moon.

Labels

They say I'll have to be on medication
For the rest of my days
To live a normal life
And to not go through another phase

So for years I haven't wondered
Around the streets for miles
My aching hips won't allow it
I guess now it's not my style

Some days I get high
Or even feel very low
My sleep is still not steady
As my mind moves to and fro

I'm not often very violent
Unless some one is aggressive towards me
I'm still in two minds to be someone's wife
As I like to be gallant and free!

So if this medication is surly
Good for my brain
I guess I don't mind it
As it takes away the pain

Some days I still struggle
Without a word to anyone else
Most days I am thankful
For the lord is my wealth.

A Million Dollars

It doesn't take a million dollars
To define and make me
I'm happy with a little cash
To keep me company

Just enough to get by
And pay the roof over my head
And the food in my tummy
And a comfy bed

To travel a bit more
And to meet al lot of friendly faces
See things I've never seen before
In some wonderful exciting places

A bit of money to help out my loved ones
And to finally be at ease
Still for now I'm a bit fortunate
As I can manage as I please

Having a million dollars
Could easily make one forget
Where they actually came from
Still I occasionally bet

For brighter days and tomorrows
Where I sometimes don't have to struggle
And give out more than I receive
Leaving my pockets in a muddle!

The Launderette

Drop your knickers and pants here
Don't matter if your straight, gay or queer
Washing your dirty under ware
And always being fair
Changing silver coins to gold
Listening to stories and secrets untold
Cleaning all the machines
Then sitting quietly with our dreams
And rather memorizing
Watching the dryers spin round and round
With clean clothes all ready for a few pound
All calming and therapeutic
Just being in a laundry
Just like watching waves crashing
In an ocean or the deep blue sea.

Feeling Fed up Again!

I don't really know how much more
I can take
He sometimes irritates me
From when I awake

If he's not at work
Which is the best place for him
After a while in my own space
I'm left feeling a bit grimme

I know it's hard for the black man
To find a steady job
But sometimes when there's no work for him
He sits around my place like a slob

He has his habits and irritations
I guess I too have mine
We rarely go out for dinner
We don't often wine and dine

Occasionally he brings me flowers
I guess that of him is sweet
I know it's difficult for both of us
We are just trying to make ends meet

For nearly 8 years we been together
Sometimes I feel I can't take no more
Sometimes I'm feeling all loved up
Sometimes I feel I'm just his hoar

I know there must be compromises
Between us there is trust
Still I need to get off this roller-coaster
For my sanity this is a must

I just can't live without him
It's difficult to live with him too
I'm glad we both got our own space
Still Just fed up with feeling blue!

When The Wind Blows

When the wind blows
On my sullen face
And I walk the streets
Fallen far from grace

When the wind blows
And I feel all alone
Even when my love
Awaits for me at my home

I sometimes wonder
If he is really there
To understand me
To care and share

But I know he does
In his own special way
Giving thanks we are together
For another day

Still when the wind blows
And I'm unsure of me
I'll sit there day dreaming
Leaning against my tree

When the wind blows
Against my scared skin
I play a melody
And I play to win.

Amsterdam Oak & Fan

I sleep on an Amsterdam oak
My comfy bed
And not always with my legs
Wide spread!

I have a fan beside me
To blow a cool breeze over me
As I'm going through the change
Very steadily

My bed is where I spend
Some of my time
Dreaming or making love
Smoking or drinking wine

It's firm and it's solid
Just like a tree
With my fan right beside me
Mr R. J Ogilvie!

A Good Day

I woke up this morning
It was a good day
I gave thanks to the Lord
For all the blessings
That come my way

For a good day to walk
A good day to dance
A good day to sing
A good day to prance

A good day to praise high
For he is great
I good to love
And not to hate

Because when you hate
It twists you up inside
Where you become bitter
and have to hide

From the Devils and demons
That drain your energy
So give thanks for your blessings
That's the remedy!

Angels

Be kind to a stranger
Because you never know
Who they may be
There could be an Angel
Walking beside you gallantly

Angels are everywhere
They may not have wings
There are some above us
We see some in our dreams

They guide us every day
They bless us from above
Angels are not full of uncertainty
Angels are full of love

So if you meet somebody
A stranger who is all alone
Just remember it could be an Angel
Fallen far, far from home.

Drum & Bass

Hearts pounding to the heavy bass
The heart beat of the world
Spiralling in space

In the universe
With heavy sound
A drum beats with our feet
firm on the ground

our feet stepping
in time with the source
until the earth
takes a different course
in space and time
bodies step and jump
to the sounds of drum and bass
where the world could flunk!

Who Are You?

Who are you?
Are you a cat or a mouse
Do you live in an apartment
Or a house
Are you fat or thin
Are you full of light
Or are you dim

Who are you?
Are you a snake
Or an ant
Do you pout
Or pant?
Who are you?
Are you friend
Or are you foe?
Do you like rain
Or snow?

Who are you?
Are you woman
Or man
Do you have a plan?

Who are we?
Are we the human race
Or are we just aliens
From space!

The Witnesses

Passing me by
With a smile on their faces
With satchel attached
From all different races

Always polite
And they say hello
To paradise they say
Is where they'll go

Where all animals and people
Will live in peace as one
Where heaven will be on earth
And everyone will become…

United in love and in unity
The witnesses are a friendly people
They are without greed or scrutiny.

The Boy from Marz

There was I in my cot
Big
Thick
Metal bars
Entrapped
The boy next to me
Was so pale and white
With goofy teeth
Whining
Like a trapped sea lion
I wondered when he would stop
His whining and crying
Made me uneasy
I waited patiently
For my new parents to come
To collect me
Eventually they came
And took me in
No more sleepless nights
From the boy with long arms
Crying next to me
The strange boy whaling
I thought
The boy from marz.

SEX

Sex is overrated.
Be kind
Be gentle
Make love
Not war!

When The Night Calls

The moon shines crescent
It is not shining whole.
It is a reminder
That in the night sky
It still shines on us
In the darkness
In our darkness
When we too
Are not feeling whole.
And then as time passes
It shines in full.
Lighting up the sky
Whilst some of us sleep
Or dance to the sounds
Of the night when it calls.

Dreams

My dreams are
Not what help me
Sleep at night
My dreams
Are what
Keep me awake

When I rest
It is not peaceful
But like a haze
Or an action packed
Adventure

Of people and places
I have never seen
Or never been
Sometimes I dream
Of my nearest
And dearest
But I do dream

My dreams are not
What help me sleep
But that
What keep
Me awake

On awaking
I may try
To decipher them
For when
I live in my reality

In the daytime
Where all is bright
Where I can
See some light
Where I still fight

My dreams
Are what keep me
Awake
For heavens sake
Just let them
Be dreams!

Warriors

Long time ago
Many, many years
There were wars
Where people lost
Their peers

Earth disaster's
Collision everywhere
Buildings fallen
warriors with matted hair

All fighting for peace
But wars never bring that
All fighting for justice
And that's a fact

As these time's haven't changed
As we are all still fighting
Instead of peace and love
Instead of uniting

There are many kinds religions
Dividing people into groups
Separating us from one another
Like a bland mushroom soup

But if that mushroom
Cloud appears?
Amid the high sky
We will all have to be warriors.
We will all have to
Come together and try
To fight, before we die…

Lacuna

I feel cold inside
Sometimes never understood
I don't fit in to
Any one brotherhood
I feel safely lost
Inside an Aladdin's cove!

Grounded Stars

Million of people walk the streets
Millions of people have their ways
Some working nine to five
Some just live in a daze

Many people are just scaping their cash
To feed their family
Many people work hard
Until insanity sets in
Always hoping for a big cash pot win

Never enough time for family
Just fitting them in a tight slot
Women working as check out girls
In a shop store
Stress men and women
Some work for the law

Many of these grounded stars
Have desires and dreams too
Like a friend who is a school teacher
But inside she is mystic blue

Another who works in a prison
Who can sing a beautiful tune
The dustbin man who is intelligent
And would love to walk on the moon

So when you walk the streets
With your pockets full
And you see a loner begging for cash
Try not to look down on them
And hurry by in a dash

As every little penny
Sees them through another day
Maybe the next time you see one of them
It could be you they give their wage!

Changing Face

Spent my childhood
Living in stress
Moving from home to home
Taken away from school
Taken away from hospital
Taken away from my parents
Taken away from clones
Of people
Who want to reach me
And strangely try
And see
What I see
Are you a cat
A vamp
A witch
Or a mouse
Tell me what house
Does your spouse
Live in?
Is he or she
God loving
Or dangerously
Full of sin?
Black is my colour
Because I can blend in
At night
Though a bit gothic
I am happy

Hip hop
And classically romantic
Some say I'm full
Of fright!
Are you an Angel
A mermaid
A fairy or
A warrior
Are you a snake
Or a demon
Warship follower?
Are there really other beings
That have changing face?
Or are we all just
A mish mash of matter
All fallen
Into earths space?
If I tell you
All that I've seen so far
Surely you would
Never become a passenger
Of my strange car
So I will let you
Guess for a while
And let you be the judge
Of me
Then maybe I get back
To you
On my own sun dial
Over a pot of English tea!

The Tree

Love is like a tree
With it's deep roots
Planted in the ground

A strong trunk
As the body
Branches reaching out
As arms with leaves on them

Giving us life
To breath it's oxygen
And with each season
Changing it's emotions
Standing tall
And sheltering us
From the heat of sun rays
Or just giving us
A cool shade

Being with us through autumn
And winter days and nights
And when the tree has shed it's leaves
For all in sight
A walk on the green Is simplicity to me
And with both hands I touch gently
With love and thanks
My tree…

Yesteryears

Just like a
Shallow stream
I awake
From
My dream

To another day
Uncertain
Of what
It may bring

I write
No longer sing
My feelings
Of yesteryears

And the smirks
And jeers
Do not bother me
At all.

Lachrymose

What it felt like
Was the pain
I would only
go through
for my children

And their cries
I smiled
And wondered
Silently
In my heart
How did they
Come
To be
From me?

Honey Bees

Little bees busy
Buzzing around
Making a buzzing sound
Around my head

Busy bees collecting nectar
From pretty flowers
And all their
Mystical powers

Busy bees buzzing around
Making an effervescent sound
Making honey
To fill my tummy

Busy bees are all well fed
And when their all gone
Surely we'll be
All dead!

When He Comes

When he comes
Will I put aside
Everything for him?

When he comes
Will he know
All of my sins?

When he comes
Shall I walk away
From my
Old life?

When he comes
Will I no longer be
Some mans
Wife?

When he comes
Do I follow him
For the rest
Of my days?

When he comes
Will my life be
Just a haze?

When he comes
Will he show
Me pure love
And understanding?

When he comes
I'll try not to be
Too demanding!

Distant Dreaming

I wasn't credited
On the day
I was born

All my father
Told me
That I was rescued
From oceans deep

And taken to steady ground
As the kingdom
Was at war

My father described
My mother
As a maiden
Filled with strife

Whose love
Ran like a waterfall
Cascading a multitude
Of colours like a rainbow

Torn between two worlds
She had captured his heart
And tend to his wounds

My father as I remembered
Was a tall gallant man
Who like the simple things
In life

And when he passed away
I too was torn between two worlds
Looking up to the heavens above
For his guidance and reassurance

Whilst searching
Ocean waves
To grasp
My mothers love.

Rainbows & Sunsets

Even when it rains
And the sun shines
There is magic
In the sky

And when the
Sun sets
There is always hope
For another day
Until we die…

Available worldwide from Amazon

www.mtp.agency

mtp.agency

@mtp_agency

Printed in Great Britain
by Amazon

27551520R00066